Getting YOUR Man to Do What YOU WANT

Six Tips for Women Who Want to Fully Enjoy Their Relationship

By Armani Valentino

b

COLLEGE BOY
PUBLISHING
"We Breed Bestsellers"

Written and Edited by **Armani Valentino**

for College Boy Publishing

Published for print & digital distribution by **Armani Valentino**

Inside Designed & Setup by **Armani Valentino**

Cover Design by **Armani Valentino**

Published in Dallas, TX, by College Boy Publishing. College Boy Publishing is a division of The College Boy Company & ArmaniValentino.com.

Copies of this book may be ordered directly from www.collegeboypublishing.com. Please allow up to 7-10 Business Days for delivery.

The author is available for keynote addresses, workshops, panel discussions, consultations, and radio & television interviews by emailing collegeboypublishing@gmail.com

Printed in the United States of America

08 09 10 11 12 MHAV 5 4 3 2 1

Getting YOUR Man to Do What YOU Want

Six Tips for Women Who Want to Fully Enjoy Their Relationship

By Armani Valentino

Dedicated to the Women

Who want to fully ENJOY their Relationship

Getting Your Man to Do What You Want

TABLE OF CONTENTS

The Purpose

Hundreds and thousands of the many women that I've met over the last 10 years always say to me, **"I have a man that I'm with... I love and believe that he loves me... However, I just can't seem to be able to get him to do the things I want."**

Coming from a man who grew up the only male in a house with three women, I always laugh when I hear this because this is quite an easy task. It is such an easy task that I will condense this mini-book in the most concise and easy to follow way, I can possibly write.

Men and women are different and we all know this. If you don't understand and accept this as absolute truth and fact, nothing that I say beyond this point will benefit you in any way, shape, form or fashion. The way we process information on a scientific level is even different. The anatomy of our bodies is different. I could go on and on about the differences, but again, this is a concise quick and easy to read guide that I wanted to make just to simplify the rest of the information that's out there and give you things that you may not have heard. I wanted to give you THE TRUTH!

If you're wondering or thinking to yourself, "What makes you an expert Armani Valentino?" I'll answer you the same way that I've done for the last five years or more, "NOTHING!" I've never called myself an expert. Other people have, but I haven't. I've been on many expert panels, shows, television and radio, colleges and universities, and I'm just sharing what I have experienced and learned from life in hopes that it may help someone else. I am national bestselling author, an Amazon.com bestseller and an Amazon International bestselling author. I've written 12 books, and I am

The Purpose

certified with the State of Texas to teach the curriculum for pre-martial/married couples known as Twogether in Texas.

But, outside of all of this, what I am is a MAN. I am a man who LOVES WOMEN and understands their role and importance in relationships, family, business, and the world at large.

Now that we are on one accord, I want you to be able to remember these things that will be on the following pages. So, **instruction #1 is to read this book 3 times**, *and then once a week on a regular basis*. Why? In order for the advice given here to actually be effective, **you must MASTER IT**. It must become a part of you.

Someone once said, "Repetition is the mother of learning and the father of skill." So, there are very easy skills and ideas that will be given here that will allow you the opportunity become better at *Getting Your Man to Do What You Want*.

TIP #1

Know What YOU Want

For many women, this seems to be the biggest issue. In order to know what you want him to do, you have to KNOW WHAT YOU WANT. You must be absolutely sure about what you want because if you're not over a period of time, he will stop doing what you're asking him to do because he feels that you'll just change up what it is that you want.

I have never seen a woman of any race, age, religion, or socio-economic background KNOW EXACTLY WHAT SHE WANTED, and not get it! **You must be clear about your desire.** Your desire must be clear in order for you to make it simple and articulate it to a man. You have to want the thing or things that you are wanting because you want them and not because someone else wants them. You can't be wishy-washy or double-minded if you want to get your man to do what you want.

In Maslow's Hierarchy of needs, the ultimate place was to be at a state of self-actualization. At this place, one is in tune with one's self, and therefore KNOWS him-SELF or her-SELF. **Know** means **to have knowledge of**. People FAIL because of LACK OF KNOWLEDGE.

Again, you can't expect someone to give you what you want if **you** don't know what you want. I promise you that once you are able to define exactly what you want, YOU WILL BE HAPPIER in YOUR RELATIONSHIP, almost overnight. Why? Because you will be more as-sured and will have taken time with YOU to search the inner workings of your own heart and mind.

HOW DO YOU FIGURE OUT
WHAT YOU WANT?

Step 1 -You have to take about 20 minutes a day to meditate, quiet your mind, and control your breathing. This helps to clear your mind of all the outside influence you get every single day. Most people want what they see other people have or want to do what they see others do. Therefore, there is very little originality. Just a whole lot of mini-me's if you know what I mean. Meditation helps you tap into your true self, and brings peace and contentment to your mind affairs and situations. Do this every day!

Step 2 – After your meditations, begin to write down what you want for your life and what you are willing to GIVE in return for that which you desire. This is a very important part of the LOVE equation. Often, women and men look for what they can give and are not able to articulate what they will give. Do this every day for 30 days and it will make a huge difference in your relationship.

Step 3 – Focus your attention only on the things you want! Often, people can easily articulate what they do not want. However, that is where it usually stops. In doing this, it causes the Universe to continue to yield to the individual what they speak of most. It is one of the laws of the Universe. So, in order to get clear with the manifestations you desire for your relationships and life in general, write down what you want and FOCUS solely on that and not the lack of what you're desiring that has not happened or showed up as of yet.

Step 4 – Stay in a positive state of expectancy. You must stay follow this step if you are to get what you're desiring. If you notice children, you cannot get them to stop expecting something that you have promised them. So much so, they will remind you of it every single time you see them. This is one of the attributes that life often beats out of people over a period of time, and that is stop expecting good to happen to and for them in their personal lives. In the area of relationships, this one intentional habit can change the trajectory of the outcome and level of happiness of the relationship.

Step 5 – Be appreciative of all things! Learning to actively and genuinely appreciate all things you have experienced and what you have in a relationship will help you to see the relationship from a more healthy space. No relationship is perfect. Therefore, being able to APPRECIATE the good that the relationship brings you will make the relationship better. Basking in the fact and matter that you have a companion with you to laugh with and talk to from time-to-time, hold & kiss, travel, go to church, and sleep side-by-side is worth appreciating on a daily basis. There was more than likely a time you wished you had someone as a companion. Appreciate all things.

TIP #2

Articulate EXACTLY What YOU Want!

Now that you have spent time focusing on your desires for what you want, you should be able to articulate what you want to the man in your life. Men are quite simple. They understand that there is no such thing as something for nothing. Well, most of us do. ;-)

When I'm selling my books or doing business at times, many women will say out of their mouth with boldness, "You should just give me that for free!" I am always perplexed at that because when I ask, "Why?" they have some of the craziest answers; such as, *"Because I'm a woman..." "Because I'm pretty..." "Because you like me..."* Or all of the other things I hear.

I don't know where this mindset comes from, but I never have seen it mentioned in any scriptures that this was the way a man was supposed to be with any woman. However, that is a whole different book. Lol...

The point is, a man understands that in order to receive he should give LOVE. The better this is understood by the woman he is in a relationship with, it produces a mutual respect and understanding of what you are asking him to do or give to you and for you! Meaning, **a man has to understand directly or indirectly what is in it for him.**

We are all creatures of habit. You are always setting up new habits or further promoting the old ones with what you articulate to him verbally and nonverbally. Men can take instructions very well; when told to them in a very simple, easy to understand way, which makes them feel good.

For example; if you want your man to kiss you, you would say to him, "Baby, I would like for you to come here and give me a kiss." It's very

direct, yet polite and it gives him instructions or directions about what you want. Another example; *"Baby, I know you're busy, but I would love for you to take out the trash to the dumpster on your way out. I've already bagged it up for you."* Same thing as the above example and you've met him halfway by initiating a part of the equation (bagging the trash). Again, these are just two examples. He may or may not do it on the first attempts. However, repetition is effective, especially when done in a positive mental attitude.

TIP #3

Don't be TOO INDEPENDENT Learn to NEED a Man

You can take what I am about to say here all the way to the bank and they will cash it for you!

"A MAN WANTS TO FEEL NEEDED."

If you are too independent, you are hurting your relationship more than you know. You always want to need your man for something. And the other part to my statement is, "BUT HE WANTS TO FEEL NEEDED FOR SOMETHING OTHER THAN MONEY!" A man wants to feel like a man.

MEN MARRY WOMEN THAT MAKE THEM FEEL LIKE A MAN. You aren't a man and will never be a man. However, if you are married, the man you married may not tell you this, but you more than likely **made him feel like a man**.

The funny thing about making a man feel like a man is that makes a woman feel like a woman. A man that feels like a man, feels strong, powerful, loved, cared about, respected, needed, and genuinely appreciated, will make a woman feel the same exact way. However, it is very hard for him to feel this way if he isn't needed for anything other than money; especially from the woman that he is in a relationship with. Needing him, also helps him not have time to stray away to another woman because he is busy TAKING CARE of the things YOU NEED HIM to be and do for you specifically.

Have you ever thought or said, "*I don't need a man!*"? If not, that's absolutely wonderful. However, many women in our society have been taught to NOT need a man. This goes against the natural tendency and desire of woman concerning men. The idea has usually been taught at an early age that must be rooted out in order for you to see the need for a man.

There is no weakness in needing a man or in a man needing a woman. We are all here for one another. Our contribution to one another is imperative for our success as humans.

Your true strength is your femininity!

Your strength as a woman is not displayed in your independence, but rather in your INTER-DEPENDENCE. Knowing and living by this principle will increase and improve your relationships with men.

TIP #4

YOU BETTA RECOGNIZE

Men like to receive awards and recognition. We like trophies, ribbons, and plaques. They remind of us what we have achieved and our ability to accomplish. WE LIVE FOR THEM!

Many people stay on a job that doesn't pay that well at times because of the awards and recognition that they receive on the job. Therefore, you will be best to have something that you give him to make him feel good and to show that you recognize and appreciate his efforts.

Always recognize the things you like and enjoy so that he will give you more of that which you reward him. That is what men are programmed to do. If you don't someone else will. And…this is not a good thing if you desire to be in a healthy relationship with a man.

WOMEN want ATTENTION FIRST & APPRE-CIATION SECOND. **MEN WANT APPRECIA-TION FIRST & ATTENTION SECOND.** You can watch my video entitled *WHY MEN AND WOMEN CHEAT* on Youtube.com where I go more in detail about this. The more you appreciate a man, the more he will want to do for you. It is when you complain, nag, and act as if he is not supposed to be recognized for "what he's supposed to do..." that he starts to tune out what is being asked of him by his woman or anyone for that manner.

Always be sure to give him an in advance notice in a very clear and precise manner of what you want or how you want something if your desires change. Doing so will allow him the opportunity to adjust to your new desire(s). Then, when he does it, be sure to recognize him, lavishly. With the oil of course...

Check out the images on the next page. They should give a great example of the above words concerning appreciation and attention.

TIP #4

A WOMAN'S HEIARCHY
ATTENTION
APPRECIATION

VS.

A MAN'S HEIARCHY
APPRECIATION
ATTENTION

TIP #5

Put That Oil On Him

In one of my relationships one of the things I would always say to her, "Put that oil on me."

That OIL is not literally OIL, but it sure feels like it to a man. It's when you talk to him in the tone and way you did in the earlier stages of the relationship when you wanted him think the best of you.

Therefore, you talked to him in your smoothest, nicest, sweetest, and/or most sexy voice that you had. It's *the voice of all of your voices that will yield you anything you want without force*. It must be mixed with the right words in order to have its full effect. But when it is, there is nothing that the man you're with won't do for you.

Another thing to do is to talk very good about him to his family and other people when you are out and about. Why? It will help him to see just how much you appreciate him, and it boosts his esteem about himself and it's directly coming from the woman with whom he is in love, YOU. This makes him feel good, and if he loves you he will transfer that right back to you in more ways than you can imagine.

King Solomon stated, "Pleasant words are as a honeycomb, sweet to the soul, and health to the bones." This is what I mean when I say, "Put that oil on him." It is one of the best tools you have when it comes to improving your relationship and getting your man to do what you want.

He also stated, "It is better for a man to live in the wilderness than in the house with a contentious and angry woman." You can speak life or death to your man, yourself, and your relationship. However, understand that you shall eat of the fruit of your tongue. Meaning, you will have that what you say, and it will manifest in your relationship, so choose the thoughts and words you speak of your man.

TIP #5

How could you improve the tone in which you speak to your man?

_____

_____

_____

_____

_____

_____

_____.

What are some genuine compliments you could give to your man, more often?

_____

_____

_____

_____

_____

_____.

TIP #6

Be PATIENT
Be NICE & Be KIND

Patience is definitely a virtue. Remember these words, "IMPATIENCE will ROB you of EVERY-THING that PATIENCE, will GIVE YOU!"

It usually takes a man longer to get his life to-gether than it does a woman. For whatever rea-son this is, it just is. It doesn't mean that there aren't men who are more stable in life than oth-ers, but generally speaking this is the case.

There are many traps and distractions out here for the average man. If he has succumbed to these, understand that much like the story of Adam in the Bible, it was probably because he was lacking wisdom and a helper in the form of a good woman to keep him from the traps set for him.

Understand also, that a man needs some time to himself just as women do. With the world we live in being extremely hectic at times, his alone time is just as important as yours. His time with his buddies is just as important as yours is with your girlfriends.

A GOOD MAN in today's time NEEDS a WOMAN that is GENUINELY NICE & KIND! If your man is nice and kind to you, it behooves you to be anything other than that to him. There are many people who hear stories about women being treated wrong, but I personally know and have my own stories of being nice to women who weren't that nice as well. What I do know is that GOOD MEN LOVE IT WHEN A WOMAN IS ALSO NICE & KIND TO THEM!

**"It's nice to be important,
but it's more important to be nice."**

Everyone wants to feel like the important one in the relationship. However, you have to under-stand that the both of you are as equally impor-tant to the relationship as the other person. Why? Because…without the other person, there is no relationship.

TIP #6

Remember the words of the Apostle Paul concerning LOVE commit them to memory and recite them aloud, daily.

Love is patient, love is kind. It does not envy, it does not boast, it is not proud.

It does not dishonor others, it is not self-seeking, it is not easily angered, it keeps no record of wrongs.

Love does not delight in evil but rejoices with the truth.

It always protects, always trusts, always hopes, and always perseveres.

From 1 Corinthians 13:4-7 NIV version of the Bible

To order more copies of this book or
others by Armani Valentino,
call
972-781-8404

Email
info@armanivalentino.com

Or visit
WWW.ARMANIVALENTINO.COM

COLLEGE BOY
PUBLISHING

"We Breed Bestsellers"

www.ingramcontent.com/pod-product-compliance
Lightning Source LLC
Chambersburg PA
CBHW060646030426
42337CB00018B/3467